# A PANDEMONIUM OF PARROTS

## and other animals

*Illustrated by* **HUI SKIPP**

B P P

Who's
upside
down?

Who's
swimming
the wrong
way?

# A COMPANY OF ANGELFISH

In neat little lines, packed in tight,
a school of fish darts left and right.
With pouting lips and bulging eyes,
they swim along the moving tide.

Who's
blowing
bubbles?

Who's not a pair?

Who's been fishing?

# A **Sloth** of **Bears**

Wrapped up warm in fuzzy suits,
they fill themselves with nuts and fruits,
then snooze the winter days away
until it's spring, when they can play.

Who's sleepy?

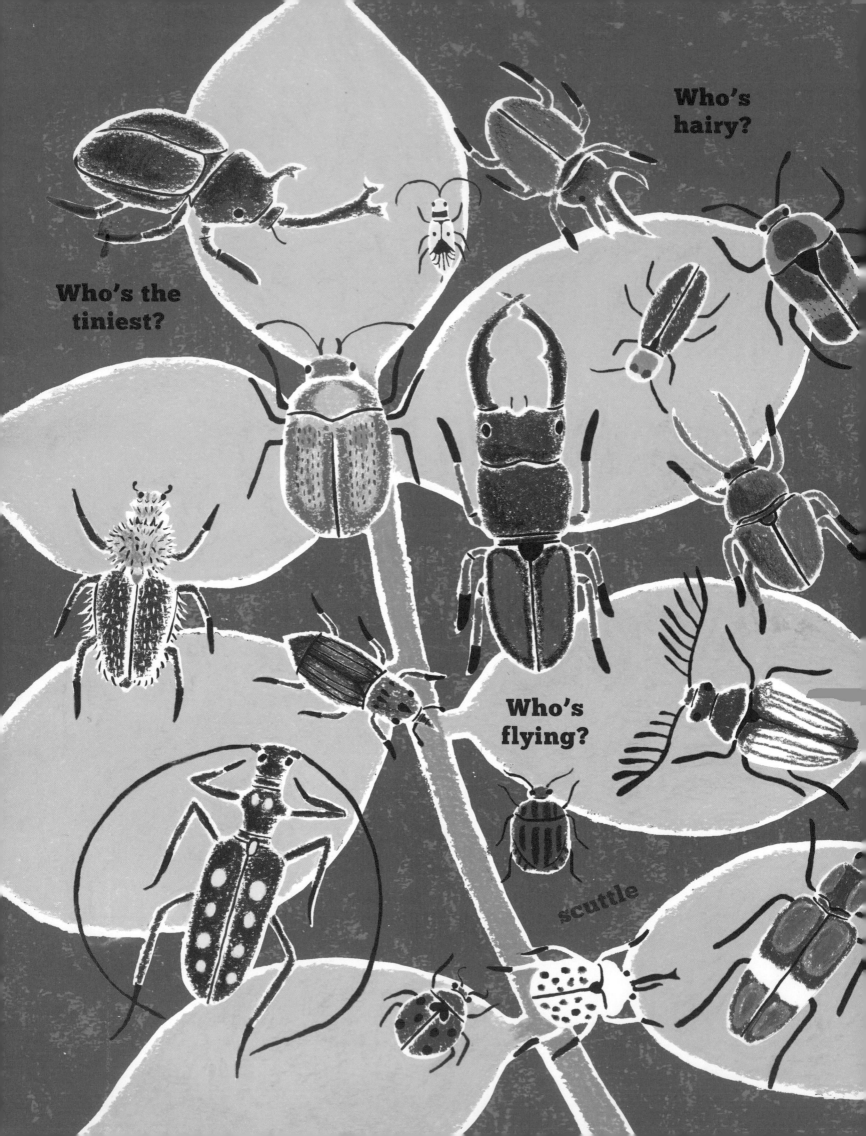

# A **PRIDE** OF **BEETLES**

With nimble legs and pinching claws,
they run across the forest floor.
Their gleaming armour shimmers bright,
while fragile wings prepare for flight.

scratch

**Who's matching?**

Who's laughing?

Who's grumpy?

# A CARAVAN OF CAMELS

They slowly cross the desert sands,
with treasures brought from distant lands.
On steady two-toed camel feet
they saunter through the searing heat.

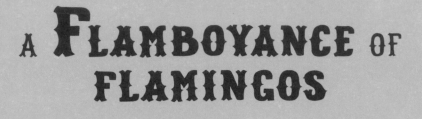

# A FLAMBOYANCE OF FLAMINGOS

See them strutting up and down
with slender legs and plush pink gowns.
Stretching their necks they honk and hoot,
then spread their wings in a proud salute.

**Who's the tallest?**

HONK

**Who's head is hidden?**

Who's peeking?

Who's got a big chin?

# AN ARMY OF FROGS

By the banks of the river an army gathers
– a funny little band of amphibian brothers.
Grinning widely from ear to ear,
they croak and sing for all to hear.

cROAk

hummmmm

Who's resting?

Who's humming?

Who's the
smallest?

chirp

A **BOUQUET** OF
**HUMMINGBIRDS**

They beat their wings as fast as light,
like tiny gems that dazzle bright.
First they hover, dive, then zoom
their fancy feathers in wondrous bloom.

Who's
upside
down?

# A CONSPIRACY OF LEMURS

They cling together in the trees
with tiny paws and furry knees.
Staring out through startled eyes,
they munch on plants and ants and flies.

Who's hitching
a ride?

Who's catching flies?

slither

# A LOUNGE OF LIZARDS

Casually they lie around
slouched on rocks or on the ground.
Suddenly one spots its prey
and in a flash it darts away.

Who's unhappy?

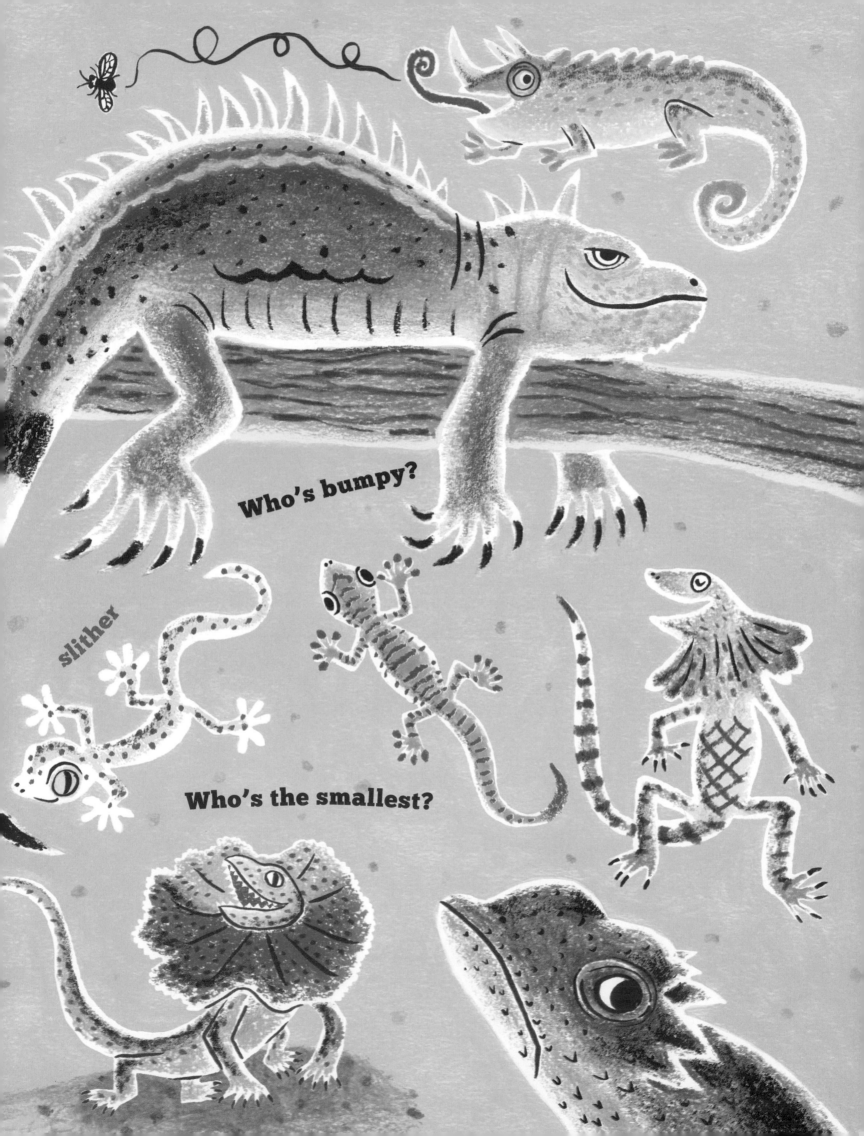

Who's bumpy?

slither

Who's the smallest?

whoop

Who's
peeping?

Who's
pointing?

# A TROOP OF MONKEYS

Funny monkeys everywhere,
tumbling and leaping through the air.
Playful, naughty, clever and wise,
they whoop and howl their jungle cries.

Who's upside down?

Who's cross?

chatter

# A PANDEMONIUM OF PARROTS

High in the forest they cackle and natter,
a glorious chorus of colourful chatter.
They swoop and glide upon the breeze,
then settle down among the trees.

kwak

Who's got blue feet?

Who's diving?

kwak

Who's hatching?

# A **HUDDLE** OF PENGUINS

Cosily dressed in feathery coats,
they snuggle together on icy floats.
Wing to wing they closely cuddle,
tapping their feet in a rhythmic shuffle.

Who's
in love?

# AN **AMBUSH** OF TIGERS

Down in the jungle they prowl around,
ready to strike in a single bound,
with giant paws and sharpened claws
and fearsome teeth in mighty jaws!

purr

Who's climbing?

Who's the youngest?

Who's roaring?

ROAR

Who's licking his paw?

baaaaa

Who's bleating?

Who's running away?

Who's scary?

# DID YOU SEE?

Take another look on every page
and see if you can find...

Who's got yellow eyes?

Who's in disguise?

Who's hiding?

**Who's peeping?**

**Who's
upside
down?**

**Who's tangled?**

**Who's
sad?**

**Who's got a
moustache?**

**Who's got a
frilly chin?**

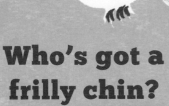

**Who's
sleeping?**

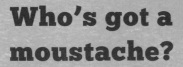

# WHO'S WHO

## A COMPANY of ANGELFISH

Some fish like to stick together in 'schools' or 'shoals' to protect themselves from predators, to search for food or to find a mate. Standing out from the crowd can be dangerous so they usually prefer the company of fish who look just like themselves.

## A CARAVAN of CAMELS

For centuries traders and travellers have used camels to cross the deserts of Asia and Africa in long trains or 'caravans'. These hardy creatures can carry heavy loads and survive a week or more without water. Their big feet help them walk across the desert terrain and their long eyelashes protect them from sand storms.

## A SLOTH of BEARS

During the cold winter months, when food is scarce, some species of bear curl up in their cosy dens and go into a deep sleep. Their heart rate slows right down and they can go for weeks and weeks without eating, drinking or even going to the toilet!

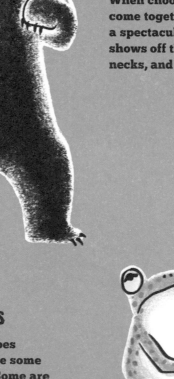

## A FLAMBOYANCE of FLAMINGOS

These graceful pink birds live and breed in large groups. When choosing a mate they come together to perform a spectacular dance which shows off their long legs and necks, and their fancy feathers.

## A PRIDE of BEETLES

Beetles come in all shapes and sizes, and they have some extraordinary talents. Some are so strong they can snap a pencil in two with their jaws, while some can glow in the dark. Others can find their way home just by looking at the stars in the sky!

## AN ARMY of FROGS

Male frogs sometimes gather in large groups around a pool and sing to attract a mate. Each species of frog makes its own special noises. Some croak or ribbit, but others whistle, cluck, click, bark, grunt, or even chirp!

## A BOUQUET *of* HUMMINGBIRDS

These pretty birds are famed for their dazzling feathers and for the humming sound they make with their wings. A hummingbird can beat its wings about 70 times per second, it can hover mid-air, fly upside down, from side-to-side and even backwards. It gets its energy by visiting hundreds of flowers every day, lapping up nectar with its long tongue.

## A PANDEMONIUM *of* PARROTS

Parrots are some of the most colourful and talkative birds on the planet. They can cackle, screech, squawk and scream, or purr like a cat, chuckle and cough. In homes they can copy the sound of a doorbell chiming, or a phone ringing and even mimic human voices. Imagine the noise a whole flock of parrots could make!

## A CONSPIRACY *of* LEMURS

Found only on the African island of Madagascar, lemurs are very clever animals. They live in small family groups and at nighttime they cuddle together in a 'lemur ball' to keep warm. When they travel around, they point their tails in the air like a flag so that everyone stays in sight.

## A HUDDLE *of* PENGUINS

During the icy Antarctic winter, while the females go in search of food, the male emperor penguins shuffle together in tightly packed groups. It is their job to look after the newly laid eggs that are tucked away above their feet. By moving forwards ever so slowly they each get their turn in the cosy centre of the huddle.

## A LOUNGE *of* LIZARDS

Each morning, these cold-blooded reptiles heat themselves up by basking in the sunshine or sitting on warm rocks. They need to warm up so they have the energy to escape predators and start feeding. Some species hunt and stalk their prey. Others sit and wait for prey to come near before catching it with their tongue.

## A TROOP *of* MONKEYS

These sociable primates show affection by cuddling, holding hands and grooming each other. Grinning or yawning on the other hand is a sign of aggression. Some monkeys have even been seen banging stones together to warn each other of nearby predators.

## AN AMBUSH *of* TIGERS

Tigers are actually solitary creatures and prefer to hunt alone. They silently stalk their prey until they're close enough to pounce. Although they are one of nature's most feared predators, many subspecies of tigers are either endangered or already extinct because of hunting and the loss of their habitats.

BIG PICTURE PRESS

First published in the UK in 2016 by Big Picture Press,
part of the Bonnier Publishing Group,
The Plaza, 535 King's Road, London, SW10 0SZ
www.bigpicturepress.net
www.bonnierpublishing.com

1 3 5 7 9 10 8 6 4 2
0516 008

ISBN 978-1-78370-462-0

Designed by Winnie Malcolm
Written and Edited by Kate Baker

Printed in China